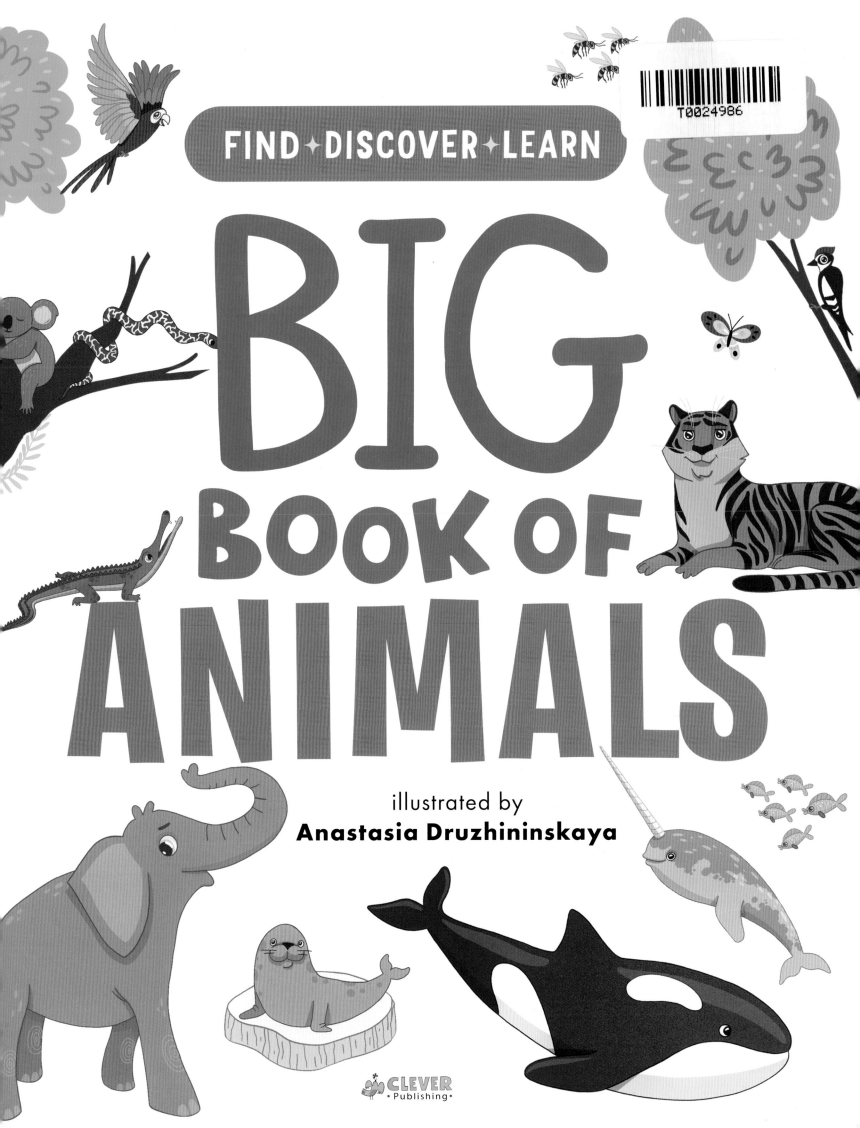

FIND ★ DISCOVER ★ LEARN

BIG
BOOK OF
ANIMALS

illustrated by
Anastasia Druzhininskaya

CLEVER
Publishing

Point to the biggest rabbit.
How many carrots
can you count?

Count all of
the mice.

Where is the smallest ant?

Find the snake.

How many worms do you see?

What color is the donkey's scarf?

How many baskets can you count?

Where is the horse who is drinking water?

Where is the sheep who is dancing?

Point to the pig wearing sunglasses.

Count the apples.

Count the bees.

What color are the flowers on the bushes?

How many woodpeckers can you find?

Find the green lizards.

Can you find the two ladybugs?

Point to the fruits and vegetables.

How many butterflies can you count?

Point to the red flowers.
Point to the yellow flowers.

Find the koala wearing
glasses.

Do you see the sleeping jaguar?

How many snakes
do you see?

Count the red-eyed
tree frogs.

How many red frogs can you find?

Can you find the crocodile with a butterfly on its snout?

Where is the baby elelphant?

Find the capybara with a bird on its back.

Which macaws are flying?

Point to the tiger with its eyes closed.

Where is the red and green chameleon?

Which owl has its eyes closed?

Can you find the airplane?

How many music notes can you count?

Point to the pigeons that are carrying letters.

How many ladybugs do you see?

Can you find the singing cardinal?

How many humps does the camel have?

Point to the two animals with large horns.

Where is the meerkat with an object on its head?

How many cacti do not have flowers on them?